Centsibility

written by **Stacey Roderick** and **Ellen Warwick**

illustrated by **Monika Melnychuk**

Kids Can Press

For Milos — SR
For Cheryl and 30 years of friendship (so far ...) — EW

We'd like to thank the following people for very generously giving us their two cents: Kathryn Fero, Arie Gula, Claire Deveau Moliner, Krista Pereira, Katie Somerville, Zoë Van't hof and Daavi Wong Wolfson. We also owe a debt of gratitude to Monika Melnychuk, and Yvette Ghione, Karen Powers and the many others at Kids Can Press for their invaluable help and support.

To my favorite sister, Andrea — MM

pLanet girL ™ is a trademark of Kids Can Press Ltd.

Text © 2008 Stacey Roderick and Ellen Warwick
Illustrations © 2008 Monika Melnychuk

Kids Can Press acknowledges the financial support of the Government of Ontario, through the Ontario Media Development Corporation's Ontario Book Initiative, and the Government of Canada, through the BPIDP, for our publishing activity.

Published in Canada by
Kids Can Press Ltd.
29 Birch Avenue
Toronto, ON M4V 1E2

www.kidscanpress.com

Edited by Yvette Ghione
Designed by Karen Powers
Printed and bound in China

CM 08 0 9 8 7 6 5 4 3 2 1

Published in the U.S. by
Kids Can Press Ltd.
2250 Military Road
Tonawanda, NY 14150

Library and Archives Canada Cataloguing in Publication

Roderick, Stacey
    Centsibility : the Planet Girl guide to money / written by Stacey Roderick and Ellen Warwick ; illustrated by Monika Melnychuk.

(Planet girl)
ISBN 978-1-55453-208-7

1. Money—Juvenile literature. 2. Finance, Personal—Juvenile literature. 3. Girls—Finance, Personal—Juvenile literature. I. Melnychuk, Monika II. Warwick, Ellen III. Title. IV. Series.

HG221.5.R64 2007   j332.4   C2007-902958-2

Kids Can Press is a *Corus* ™ Entertainment company

Contents

Charity

Words to the soon-to-be money wise

Some people think money makes the world go 'round. Others think it's the root of all bad things. And, of course, there's that saying that a fool and her money are soon parted ... Yep, there's a lot to say about it, but what do you really know about money?

Well, most of us know how to spend it. Want to take a bus to your friend's place? You need money. Want to go to the movies? You need money. Want a snack from the vending machine at school? You need ... you know what. And these are just the little expenses. What about yoga classes and digital cameras? They don't come cheap! It's tough to get by without needing to spend some money now and then.

So if you're going to spend money, you need to know how to make it. If you make it, you should know how to save it. And once you have it, well, it's pretty great to be able to share it. A money-smart girl needs to know it all: how to make it, save it, spend it and share it.

Get comfy and get reading for lots of ideas for improving your cash flow. Then learn some pain-free ways of saving that hard-earned dough for the bigger stuff while still indulging your inner fashionista (or whatever your guilty pleasure happens to be). And you might wonder what there could possibly be to learn about spending money — that part's a cinch, right? Well, check out some tricks to help you not just shop, but shop smart. You'll pick up some tips for making a little go a long way and making nothing go an even longer way. And you'll discover why a truly rich girl is one who shares her riches.

The more you know about managing your money, the easier it will be to make the choices that you want to make, do the things that you want to do, and rule your own world — cents-ibly!

MAKE IT

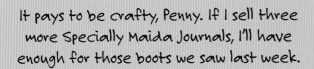

It pays to be crafty, Penny. If I sell three more Specially Maida Journals, I'll have enough for those boots we saw last week.

REALLY?

I know a super-fast way to double the money you already have, Maida.

YEP, just fold it in half!

It really doesn't grow on trees

You're no fool — you know money can't buy happiness. But since you don't live under a rock, you also know that there are lots of things it can buy — things you really need and things you just really want. You use money to buy school supplies (need 'em), download your favorite tunes (want 'em), save for college (need to), shop for the latest styles (want to) ... and the list goes on. Lucky for you, there are ways to line your pockets with some extra cash: You can earn an allowance, do odd jobs, get an after-school or weekend job or even start your own business.

Wanna get on the path to making some cash? Read on for lots of tips and advice on becoming a moneymaker.

QUIZ: The herstory of money

Whether you think of yourself as a money master or a bit of a dough dodo, you might just learn a thing or two by taking this quick true-or-false quiz.

1. The word money comes from the name of a goddess.

2. You can find the faces of Susan B. Anthony, Sacagawea and Martha Washington on American paper currency.

3. There are no Canadian-born women on regular-circulation Canadian coins.

4. Female or male, workers have always made the same money for the same kind of work.

5. As a group, girls ages 12 to 17 have a whole lotta buying power.

ANSWERS

1. **True.** The word money comes from Moneta, one of the names of Juno, a Roman goddess. The story goes that the honking of her geese warned the ancient Romans of an attack. To show their gratitude, they built a temple in her honor, which later became a mint (a place where money is made).

2. **False.** Susan B. Anthony and Sacagawea both appear on U.S. dollar *coins*, but Martha Washington is the only woman whose portrait has appeared on U.S. paper currency. Her face appears on the $1 Silver Certificates of 1886, 1891 and 1896.

3. **True.** Queen Elizabeth II appears on most Canadian money, but she was born in London, England. There *is* a 1994 Anne of Green Gables $200 commemorative gold coin, but as much as we love her, Anne is a fictional character, not a real woman.

4. **False.** In fact, laws had to be passed to make sure that women and men were paid equally. In 1956 the Canadian government passed the *Female Employees Equal Pay Act*, and in 1963, the U.S. Congress passed the *Equal Pay Act*. Shockingly, women still make less on average than the men who do the same job! Fortunately that gap is getting smaller each year.

5. **True.** According to a 2005 study of U.S. teens, girls spend more money weekly than boys. This means girls have real spending power! And since advertisers know this and will do what they can to get you spending on the stuff they're selling, do yourself a favor and use your power wisely!

Making your own money makes sense

Maybe you haven't really thought about making your own money or think it sounds like too much work or even a bit scary. But there are loads of good reasons for deciding to earn your own.

✱ Imagine never again having to ask your parents for cash for the movies or to buy your best friend the perfect birthday present. In a word, earning your own money gives you some *independence.* If it's your money, you have a say in how to spend it.

✱ It's especially smart for girls to have good money sense. As you saw in the quiz, some companies still pay men more money than women who do the same job. Unfair? You bet! But the more money-savvy you are now, the more likely you are to know how much your work is worth later (which is at least as much as the other guy).

✱ Working can boost your confidence as well as your bank account. How? Well, chances are you'll have to learn a new thing or two when you do more work around the house, get a job or start your own business. The more you test yourself, the more you'll realize you can do. The more you know you can do, the more you'll believe in yourself.

✱ Since life really isn't like the movies or a fairy tale, it's pretty unlikely that someone will come along and take care of you for the rest of your life. But the good news is that by earning your own money and controlling your financial future, you're much more likely to live happily ever after.

✱ While adding to your bank account, you can also add to your social life. Having a job or running your own biz is a guaranteed way to make new pals.

✱ Keep an eye on the future (c'mon, it's not that far away); the jobs you have now can teach you a lot about what you might want — or might *not* want — in a career.

Once you decide it's time you had some of your own money to manage, let your parents in on your plan. After all, you'll need them onside, and they'll likely have some good advice for you. Let them know why you think it's a good plan to have some cash of your own and what your ideas are for making money. They can help you figure out what kind of work is right for your age, how much time you can spare for moneymaking, what job would suit your talents and strengths, and other stuff that will help you find the right route to more loot.

At-home earner

You or your parents aren't comfortable with you getting a job yet? No problem! There are more than a few ways to make some moolah without joining the job market.

Pocket money

The most common way to make some spending money is to earn an allowance. If you aren't already getting one, this might be an option. Or maybe you've already been getting one but think it's time for a raise. Either way, here are some things you'll want to discuss with the source of your allowance — your folks.

✱ What chores are you willing to do to earn your allowance? What are the consequences if you don't live up to your end of the bargain? Or what if you go above and beyond what you agreed to by doing extra chores now and then? Will you get a bonus?

✱ How much money will you get and how often? Your parents will probably have the most say about this, but you can make suggestions. Ask your friends how much they get (and what they do in exchange) as a way of figuring out a reasonable amount for you. If you think your parents' offer is a little behind the times, keep a money journal (see page 60) for a week and then show them the facts. If you're already on the parental payroll, this might help you negotiate a raise. And if you have a good track record — you've been doing everything you agreed to do without being told fifty times — it won't hurt to remind them. You can also suggest what payment schedule would help you best manage your money: getting paid every week, every two weeks or every month.

✱ Although your allowance is your own hard-earned money, your parents might want to suggest ways to use it. For instance, they might want you to put 10% (or $1 out of every $10) away as savings. This might seem like a drag, but it's actually a great idea. (You'll find lots of reasons why in the Save It section.) Just hear them out.

The most important thing to remember is to keep your cool — hissy fits never solve anything. And if you need to, bend a little. So you have to empty the dishwasher every night and your friend who gets a bit more allowance doesn't. It's not the end of the world, and it's still money in your pocket.

Wanna make it really official? Make yourself an allowance contract. Write out everything you and your parents agreed to. Then you each read, sign and date it.

Odd jobs, etc.

Getting an allowance isn't the only way to make a bit of spending money. Try thinking about jobs around the house that adults never seem to get around to (or complain about): rolling pennies, shining shoes, sewing on buttons, cleaning out the garage, downloading and organizing the photos from the digital camera, polishing the silverware, etc. You can strike a deal with your parents, other family members or close neighbors: For every chore you do, you get paid the fee you discussed before you did the job. It's a win–win situation!

Another way of feeding your piggy bank is to get your parents' okay to ask relatives for cash gifts for birthdays and holidays. And if you're saving for something really special, you might ask your parents to match the money you earn, which means that for every dollar you get, your parents pay you the same amount. This way you really will double your money (unlike Penny Pincher's trick)!

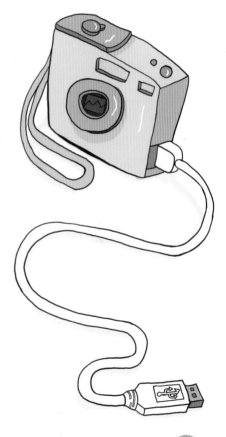

Working girl

You've talked to your parents, and you all agree you are ready for a job outside of the house? Great! Now, here are some things to think about when you're picturing yourself in the working world.

✳ Is there something that you're really passionate about or that you think might be in your future as a career? Mad for horses and dream of becoming an equestrian gold medalist? Maybe there's a job at your riding school mucking out the stables. (Hey, even Oprah had to start off small.) A job doing something you love or are curious about can help you make decisions about what subjects to take in school or what career path you want to follow.

✳ Is this the right job for you? Can't pry your eyes open until the last possible minute on school days? A morning paper route probably isn't for you, then. Read job ads carefully and really think about what will be expected of you. There's no need to take a job that makes you miserable or that just doesn't suit your personality.

✳ What are the hours? Is your schedule packed with soccer practices and homework? What about the time you want to spend hanging out with your friends? A job can really cut into your after-school and weekend time.

✳ Ready to deal with the not-so-fun parts of having a job? For example, what if you're having one of those days and just don't feel like smiling brightly at your customers? That's no excuse to ditch. Your employer expects that you will turn up and do your job as well as you can (unless you're really sick, of course).

The job market

There are laws about how old you must be to be hired by a business. Basically, the government gets that your education is super important, and they don't want you out working when you should be in school learning. It depends where you live, but in many places you have to be at least fourteen to be hired for a part-time job — and even then you can work only so many hours and at certain times of the day. There are places where you can work when you're twelve, but doing only certain kinds of jobs and with written permission from your parents. Employers will know what the rules are where you live, but you can also ask your parents to help you research the laws.

So if you're under fourteen, there probably aren't jobs in a clothing store or fast food joint for you just yet. But do your research by asking around, checking bulletin boards at the community center and the library, reading the classifieds of your local paper, etc. There will probably be some jobs you *can* apply for, especially in the summer. What about becoming a newspaper or flyer deliverer, junior camp counselor, park or pool concession-stand attendant or even an actor? Ads for these jobs should say how old you have to be to be hired. If not, look for a number to call so you can ask.

To apply for a job, you'll have to fill in an application. When you pick up your application, make sure to look like you've made an effort. We know people shouldn't be judged on their appearances, but you can't blame an employer who's put off by chipped nail polish and a grubby tank top. And having the right attitude is just as important — be sure to be polite and try to give off your most positive vibes.

If you can, take your application home so you can take your time with it. Often it's the first impression you'll make on your boss-to-be, so you'll want to be sure that it's neat. If you don't understand something, ask for help rather than trying to guess. Most employers aren't looking for a sample of your creative writing skills. And remember to check it (or even better, get someone else to check it) for spelling mistakes!

Next, you get a call for an interview — congrats! Interviews can be a bit nerve-wracking, for sure, but one way to keep yourself from freaking out is to prep beforehand. Everything's less scary when you feel prepared. Try thinking carefully about what might be expected of you if you get the job, or have a pretend interview with a friend or family member.

Some typical interview questions are: What can you tell me about yourself? How would your teachers describe you? Why do you want this job? What are your strengths? This is your chance to show an employer that you have what they are looking for: the personality, the skills, the enthusiasm, etc. Keep this in mind when you're thinking about your answers.

Another way of quieting those nervous butterflies is to remember to keep breathing. Sounds obvious? You'd be surprised what a few good, deep breaths before you walk into that interview can do!

Be sure to arrive for your interview on time, looking smart and being polite and positive. Keep up your smile and look people in the eye when you are speaking. Good eye contact like this shows that you're confident and that you believe in what you are saying. You know you've got what it takes — now's your chance to show it!

Mizz Biz

Question: What if you're not old enough for a job at the mall, or you need to work around your karate class schedule, or you'd just rather be your own boss?

Answer: You can become an entrepreneur. (Entrepreneur is a fancy way of saying "someone who starts and runs his or her own business.") By running your own business, you have your independence, you can take on as much or as little work as you like and you get some great experience. Being an entrepreneur can mean running a garage sale or lemonade stand now and then, or it can mean starting a business you plan to work at for a while.

Entrepreneurial Spirit Checklist

❑ Are you creative? Have you spotted a need that could be filled? Or have you figured out a way of making your business unique?

❑ Do you love what you do? Your best bet is to build a business around something you really enjoy 'cuz you'll be doing a lot of it.

❑ Are you determined to ride the highs and lows of being in business for yourself? You've gotta have faith in yourself and your abilities, even when things get a bit bumpy.

❑ Do you have lots of energy? Getting a company up and running is hard work, and entrepreneurs often work harder than people who report to a boss. (It's no coincidence that "busy" is the root word of "business.")

❑ Are you organized? Love making lists? Worship the inventor of the label maker? Then you're in luck because successful businesses are organized businesses!

Girl Inc.

So now that you know you've got what it takes and your parents are on board, what's a smart and talented girl to do? Are you going to sell things you make (also known as selling goods) or get paid for your skills (also known as offering a service)? This chart might give you an idea or two.

IF YOU LOVE ...	TRY ...
academics or languages	tutoring
animals	dog walking or washing; pet sitting
baking	putting together treat-filled gift baskets
beading	making jewelry and accessories
blogging	publishing a 'zine
computers	doing Internet research; designing Web pages
crafts	making dolls, puppets or birdhouses
doodling	making hand-drawn cards
kids	babysitting; being a birthday party clown
knitting or sewing	making clothing and bags
plants or the outdoors	plant sitting; doing yard work
music	DJing

As smart and as talented as you are, when you start a business, you need to be sure that you know as much as you can about your product or service. Gonna be the most popular babysitter in your 'hood? First take a babysitting course. Wanna be the next best thing since sliced bread and Rachael Ray all rolled up into one? Be sure to test all your recipes — a few times. (We're pretty sure your little brother won't mind being your guinea pig.)

Making it your business

Whether you're a crafty girl who wants to sell stuff you make or you've decided to turn that helpfulness into some extra cash, you mean business.

Once you have your business idea, you get to name it. The name should say something about the business in a way that also says something about you. Have some fun with it and come up with something catchy — you want your customers to remember it.

Next, you might need some start-up money. This is what you'll need to spend to get your biz going. How much you need will depend on your costs. Some of your costs will be what you'll need to spend to make your product — ingredients or materials — or provide your service — equipment or transportation. Setting up shop might be another cost. You might be able to get permission to work out of your locker at school or out of your home (no money needed!). But if you have something to sell, you might decide that a fabulous display is the best way to show off — and sell — your products. Sometimes it costs money (a rental fee) for a booth at craft fairs, but it's often free or pretty inexpensive to sell your stuff at community fairs or church bazaars. Before you sign any agreement, read it through carefully with your parents and make sure to ask about the fees.

To keep your start-up costs low, think about what's already available to you. Do you have some of the equipment you'll need? Not afraid to ask for favors? Borrow a rake and wheelbarrow to begin with for your lawn-care business. What are the cheapest materials you can use without hurting the quality of your product or service? Are you a DIY diva? Build your own screens for making handmade paper.

A great, no-risk — and free! — way to find customers is to use word of mouth (friends who tell friends who tell friends, and so on). Tell everyone you know. If they don't need your products or services, they may know people who do. But if you want to reach more people quickly, you can advertise.

Advertising doesn't have to cost a lot, but you might need to pay to print flyers, put an ad in your community paper, have someone design a Web page (if you aren't computer savvy yourself), etc. Create a design that's eye-catching but also easy to read. Include all the information you want people to have: the name of your business, what your business offers, your rates (or at least the promise of reasonable rates), your qualifications

(courses you've taken, glowing quotes from people), what makes your service stand out (who else makes organic chocolate chip cookies?) and how to find you (your home phone number and your Web site should do it). Be sure to run all of your advertising by your folks. And no one's perfect, so ask someone else to proofread your Web site, poster or ad for any mistakes (and even to double-check your phone number).

Ask if you can put up posters at school, the library, the community center, the grocery store or anywhere else in your neighborhood that has a bulletin board. Cut a fringe across the bottom of your poster and write your business's name and number on the tabs you've made. People just rip off a tab and voilà — they have your number.

If you're selling a product, it's a good idea to keep a list of everything you make. If you can, take photos, too, and put them in a funky little album or post them on your Web site. Ta-da! You've made yourself a catalog. If you run out of something, customers can still see what you make and order it from you. It's a good reminder for you, too.

Of course, when we dream, we usually dream big. But when you're just starting out, it's a good idea to start on the small side, especially if you're not sure how big your market (the number of possible customers) is. If for some reason you have a hard time selling your goods, then you don't want to lose the money that you spent making them. If you sell out quickly, you'll know for sure that there's a demand (people want to buy your products) and you can make more the next time.

And remember the third point on the Entrepreneurial Spirit Checklist? If your first try at your business is disappointing, don't give up! You might just need to think more about how to make your products or services more appealing to your customers. Heck, why not ask them what did and didn't work and what you can do to make it better? Or maybe you need to give more thought to your advertising. Are there other ways to let people know about your business? Are you reaching the people who you think will be interested in your business?

The price of doing business

Whether you're a one-woman assembly line or your business is offering a service (with a smile, of course), you need to decide how much to charge your customers. It is a business, after all!

If you've got goods to sell, first figure out how much the materials you need to make each item cost. For example, for her Specially Maida Journals, Ms. Money uses the scrap paper from her mom's home office and buys the rest of her supplies in bulk at a discount store. She spends $16 on enough materials to make four journals. She does some easy math ($16 ÷ 4) and figures out that it costs her $4 to make each journal.

Next, you'll need to figure out what your profit (the amount of money you want to earn for each item) is going to be. Now, don't get greedy — you also need to look around and see what others are charging for similar items. You can't charge more than people are willing to pay. Back to Maida — she does her research and finds out that the least expensive journals at the mall are $11. Her journals are handmade, so they take more time to make than the factory-made ones from the mall. Still, she figures if she prices her journals at $10 a pop, that's a little less than the competition but she'll still make $6 on each journal that she sells.

Another thing to think about when calculating your profit is how much time it takes to make your product — time is money, as the saying goes. For example, if Maida took two hours to make each journal, she would make $3 per hour ($6 profit ÷ 2 hours of work = $3 for 1 hour). But since Maida has had lots of practice making her journals, it takes her only an hour to make one. That means she makes $6 per hour. Not exactly the big bucks, but not bad either, especially since she loves making her journals and is able to sell them as fast as she makes them.

$10

$10

If you want to make some money by walking dogs or providing some other service, you can choose one of two ways to charge your customers:

✱ An hourly rate — this means you'll be paid for every hour you work. If you're charging by the hour, remember to keep an eye on the time.

✱ A flat rate — this means you'll charge a fixed price for the whole job, no matter how long it takes. If you go this route, make sure you really understand what the job needs because you don't want to under- or overcharge.

Like Maida did for her journals, you'll need to do your research — what's the going rate, and how do others charge for the same service? Once you figure that out, decide whether you have room to charge a little less to give yourself a competitive advantage (in other words, a customer might choose you because your price is a bit better). Not too much lower, though, because your time is valuable, too. Also, charging too little can work against you — people might assume your services aren't as good as others'. The nice thing about being your own boss is that you make the decisions, so when it comes to talking about prices, you can also be open to a bit of bargaining (as long as you don't walk away feeling like you've been taken for a ride).

Biz whiz!

Finding and keeping customers is going to be the key to your success. You know that advertising is the way to find them, but how do you keep them? Once you have a customer or ten, you need to make sure they are happy. When you offer excellent quality (of course!) or do a great job (always!), a customer will be quick to use you again and to pass your name on to others — it's that word of mouth thing again. Getting a good name for yourself is the easiest way to drum up business!

And keep thinking of more ways to make your biz the best. Can you offer anything that other people don't or sweeten the deal? For example, if you're a dog walker, what about offering a free dog wash for every ten walks? You can also keep customer files with their contact info and notes that might help you customize your service. One of your customers is nutty for nuts? E-mail her when you come out with your new Plenty o' Pecans Pie. And make sure your customers know that they have your ear. The best way to make your customers happy is to give them what they want (as long as it's a reasonable request, of course). A happy customer is a repeat customer!

Keeping track

However you make your money, it's always smart to keep track of your cash flow (the money you're spending and the money you're bringing in). Use your money journal (see page 60) or a spare notebook to jot it all down. If you don't, you'll be amazed at how little you have to show for all your hard work. (Somehow it's easier to spend if you aren't paying attention.)

Your records will come in handy, especially if (when!) your business is booming. That's because if you make over a certain amount, you may need to pay taxes. Tax is money you pay the government, which then uses it to help run the country. Taxes are a percentage of the amount of money you make in a year. The more you make, the more tax you pay. Ask your parents to help you find out if you owe the government. You should be able to find all the information you need from your government's taxation and revenue Web site.

On-the-job safety

Last, but definitely not least, your safety is way-y-y more important than any amount of money you make. Keep these rules in mind when you're working:

✱ Pay close attention during any safety training you are given at work. These aren't just a bunch of silly rules — you're learning to keep yourself and others as safe as possible. Feel like you missed something? Ask questions 'cuz this stuff is important!

✱ If your work means going to people's homes, make sure that your parents know the names of the people you are working for, their addresses and phone numbers, and how long you expect to be there. (Be sure to call your folks if you're going to be longer than you first thought.)

✱ If your biz takes you somewhere you've never been before, bring a parent or adult friend with you.

✱ Never go door-to-door alone, and deal with strangers only when you are in a public place.

✱ If you have a cell phone, take it with you when you're working.

✱ Always go with your gut. If someone is making you feel uneasy, leave that situation or tell whoever is in charge. Don't worry about being rude or embarrassing yourself — an adult should understand.

Girl entrepreneur

When she was eleven years old, Lizzy Solomon came up with a business idea: She wanted to create a stationery line like no others she'd seen. What was going to make these cards and calendars unique? They would reflect kids just like Lizzie — kids with disabilities who like to have fun. Working with an artist who is a family friend, Lizzy started Lizzy's Lines™. The Nashville, Tennessee, native has even won awards for her business savvy. And not only does Lizzy have a good head for business, but she also has the heart for it, too — a portion of her company's profits is donated to Easter Seals.

Pretty paper beads

Talk about low start-up costs!
Jewelry made out of old magazines
or wrapping paper is cheap
to make, but chic enough to sell.

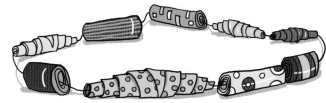

• colorful magazine pages, wrapping paper or origami paper

• straws (regular or extra skinny)

• embroidery floss or anything else you want to use for stringing

• a ruler, scissors, white craft glue

1 Measure, mark and cut triangles that are about 2.5 cm (1 in.) across the bottom and about 25 cm (10 in.) high. Each triangle will make one bead.

2 Place a triangle right side (the side you want to show) down on the table. Spread a thin layer of glue on the triangle.

3 Lay the straw along the wide end of the triangle. Roll the triangle tightly around the straw.

4 To finish the bead, add a bit more glue to the tip of the triangle and hold it in place until the glue dries.

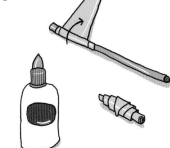

5 Cut the straw around the bead, as close to the edge of the paper as possible.

6 Repeat steps 2 to 5 until you have as many beads as you want.

7 String your beads on floss or string, and cut the right length for a necklace, bracelet or anklet.

ADDED VALUE

✱ For longer beads, make wider-bottomed triangles.

✱ For shorter, rounder beads, make narrower-bottomed triangles.

✱ For tube-shaped beads, cut rectangular strips instead of triangles.

SAVE IT

Keeping your eyes on the prize

You've heard that saving some moolah is a good idea, but what's the inside scoop on stashing your cash? And why bother, anyway? It's more fun to spend than to save, right? Well, that ain't necessarily so. If you think buying a new pair of shoes gives you a warm fuzzy feeling, it can be even warmer and fuzzier to look at a pile o' cash and know that you've got it all in the bag. Not convinced? Just check out this section to get the goods on saving your goods. Find out what the 10% solution is, figure out that a goal isn't just something that happens in a soccer game, and find out what's so interesting about interest.

QUIZ: What's your money purse-onality?

If getting started makes your knees knock, get the quivers under control by trying out this quiz to see where you're starting from. Check out the scenarios below and choose the answer that sounds most like you. Then add up your As, Bs and Cs to find out what money type you are.

1. Your best pal lost her lunch money. You:

a) Figure it's a good way for her to learn to take better care of her money.

b) Loan her some cash to join you in the lunch line at school.

c) Take her out for a fancy lunch — your treat.

2. At the mall, you see slippers perfect for your friend's birthday present — and they're on sale to boot! But you're trying to save for a new bike. What do you do?

a) Unless they're on sale for 100% off (as in free), there's no way you're putting off your new bike.

b) It's a good sale and your friend will love them, so you go for it. You'll pick up a few extra babysitting jobs to make up the money for your bike.

c) You can't pass up a great sale like this, so you buy them for your friend and pick up a pair for yourself, too!

3. Your classmate Jimmy hasn't paid back the money he borrowed from you. He says he needs to borrow just a little more, but promises to give it all back soon. You:

a) Say *No way!* and vow never to loan money to anyone again. Ever!

b) Tell him the first loan left you a little strapped for cash. Offer to help him find other ways to come up with the money he needs.

c) Figure he's good for it — you know he has an after-school job, and it's only money! Being generous is a virtue.

4. It's Sunday morning, and a local charity is at the door looking for a donation. You:

a) Explain that you've got other plans for your hard-earned money.

b) Say no, but offer to volunteer for them sometime.

c) Empty your wallet into their donation box. They can surely use it more than you, right?

5. Your teacher just announced a class ski trip. You've always wanted to ski, but it's going to cost quite a bit. You:

a) Skip the trip and save your money. It'll probably be really fun but once it's over, you won't have anything to show for the money you spent.

b) Go for it! Use some of your savings and ask your parents for an advance on your allowance for the rest. You can live a little more cheaply for the next couple of months to make up the money, which is better than missing the trip of the year.

c) Beg, borrow or steal. You'll do whatever you need to do rather than miss out on a good time!

ANSWERS

Mostly As: You're a champion cheapskate. There's nothing wrong with keeping a keen eye on your money, but not at the expense of missing out on fun stuff or being stingy with people you care about. You might want to loosen those purse strings a little.

Mostly Bs: You're right on the money. Being a great money handler means making smart decisions about what's right for you and what's right for other people. Most good decisions will fall somewhere in between.

Mostly Cs: You're a spendthrift, not a thrifty spender. It's great to have fun with your money and be generous, but it's not so great to be totally broke when you really need some dough. Try keeping a tighter grip on your wads of cash.

Savings = choices

Saving may sound like a bit of a bore, but it definitely isn't boring to be able to buy something you want when you want it. Saving is really about making and having choices. If you make the choice to put some cash away for a rainy day, you'll have choices when that day comes — and it will come! Saving is kind of like planning to be spontaneous. So when your friend calls you up and asks if you want to see the C-Notes on Saturday night, you'll have the cash to dip into to go. But if you don't have the cash saved, well, you can't, now can you?!

Saving counts for the big choices, too. Having money in the bank means that when you're ready, you can put it toward college tuition fees, travel or a move across the country and make all kinds of other choices about how your life is going to go. Putting a little away now — and maybe skipping that little something you want today — means there might be a bigger payoff later on. Check out these savings tips for a heads-up.

The 10% solution

It's not glamorous, it's not mysterious, but this is the best savings secret there is! If you save 10% of whatever you earn in your lifetime, you'll always have what you need. The idea is to pay yourself first: Before you spend any money that you get, add 10% of it to your savings. Say you get an allowance of $10 a week. Saving 10% would mean putting away $1 a week. Once you get in the habit, you'll get used to making do with a little bit less, and you won't even notice the difference. A dollar may not seem like a lot, but at the end of the year you'll have fifty-two bucks saved. And if you're used to living on $9 a week, it'll feel like found money!

The What if? fund

Also known as the eek!, whoops! or rats! fund, an emergency stash of cash is something everyone should have — at any age. There are the expenses you can expect in the future, like birthday gifts for friends and family, or a bus pass, and then there are the "what ifs" — the things that'll take you by surprise, like concert tickets (eek!), paying for that broken something (whoops!) or replacing your lost bus pass (rats!). You can build your emergency fund using the 10% solution, then once you have enough to cover your butt, set it aside and don't touch it unless the situation is dire. If you do need to dip into it, replace the money as soon as you can. So whether it's for something unexpected and exciting, or something unexpected and distressing, having a stash of cash to pay for it will make life a lot less stressful. You don't want to be caught cents-less!

Outta sight!

Ever notice how easy it is to spend money when it's in your pocket or purse? Just knowing it's there can give you the urge to splurge and can make it easier for you to fall for fancy advertising. If one of the simplest ways to save is to not spend (duh!), it's safe to say that if you don't have the money with you, you can't spend it. Carry only what you need. If you see something you want but can't buy it, that itch to spend will clear up on the spot. The funny thing about impulse shopping (buying something you didn't plan to) is that most of the time, when you get home and really think about it, that little something that you thought looked so amazing in the store suddenly doesn't look so amazing — and you don't actually want it. This is what's called "buyer's remorse" — instead of feeling warm and fuzzy about your latest buy, you just regret it. So when Grandma gives you fifty bucks for your birthday, put it away! Stick it in your savings spot until you decide whether to spend it and what to spend it on.

Goals: Not just for sports

The first step in savings goal setting is to dream big. What do you really wish you had or could afford? This is reach-for-the-stars, dare-to-imagine time. So what's it going to be? A summer drama or dance workshop or computer camp, a surfing trip in Hawaii or a car when you turn sixteen? Divide your wish list into the nows — stuff you want sooner rather than later — and the thens — stuff you want later in life.

The next step is to come back down to Earth a bit. Read through your lists and sort the nows and thens according to how much you want each item.

Then start at the top of the now wish list and make a plan to get that thing by figuring out:

❋ How much it costs. Make sure to add in the sales tax, if any. Think about added costs, too: If you're saving for an mp3 player, you'll probably have to buy some music. Or if you're saving for a cell phone, you'll have to budget for the monthly fees. Be sure to shop around for deals. (See the Spend It section on how to be a savvy shopper.)

❋ Whether you need or just want it. In other words, how long can you wait?

❋ Where the money will come from. Can you trim your weekly expenses by walking to school instead of taking the bus? (Excellent exercise anyway!) Bring your lunch from home instead of buying it? Do you really need that daily soda fix? How much of your allowance can you save each week to put toward your goal? Do you get birthday or holiday money? Is there a job you could do after school or on weekends to make some extra cash?

Okay — you're ready to make a savings plan. First, figure out how much money you have and how much you'll be getting in the near future. Then work out what you need for your goal. Now it's math time! (Don't worry if you're not a math whiz — it's pretty basic stuff, and a trusty calculator will get you through in a snap!)

This is what Penny Pincher's plan looks like.

GOAL: To learn how to play the guitar.

GUITAR: A new one costs $300, but a used one costs only $150. Used it is!

Savings in piggy bank	$48
Birthday next month	+ $50 from Grandma & Grandpa
	+$25 from Aunt Katie
Total saved	$123

Guitar	$150
	– 123 saved
	$27 still needed

Weekly allowance	$15
	– $6 spending money & savings
	$9 per week

$27 ÷ $9 = 3 weeks to save for
the rest of the guitar money,
and it's a done deal (yeah!)

LESSONS: $16 per week — a deal offered by Maida's older brother, and Mom will pay for half (thanks, Mom!), so it's only $8 per week.

Weekly allowance	$9
	– $8 lessons
	$1 leftover for weekly savings

Now Penny's strumming sweetly and still has some savings for future gigs, too. That rocks!

The how and the where

Now that you know why saving is a great idea, are you feeling inspired to save? Oh yeah! All set to plan out your savings goals? You want it and you're gonna get it! The next step is the how and the where. How do you put your plan into action? How do you keep track of it? And where do you put your hard-earned stash while it's growing?

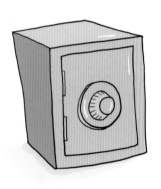

Get in the groove

Wouldn't it be amazing if there were some magical way of saving that was as easy as waving your wand? Well, hate to break it to ya, but there's no magic to it. Still, there is something you should know that will make saving a lot easier: Saving is a habit, not a skill. That means you don't need any special abilities to save. It's not a talent you're born with, like being great at math or sports. Anyone can be a great saver! Once you get in the groove of making saving a regular thing, like using the 10% solution, it's a cinch. Saving can become as much of a habit as brushing your teeth or making sure your bus money is in your pocket every morning — something you don't really think about, you just do it automatically. That's when it gets super easy and your savings will grow super fast!

Track your loot

Once you've worked out what you're saving for and where the savings are coming from, you'll want a way to tend your tender, or keep track of your savings. There are a few ways to do this — check them out on the opposite page. Or you might figure out your own way to keep track. However you do it, it'll for sure inspire you to keep going when you see your savings grow.

GRAPH IT

It's simple to draw a savings graph to keep an eye on your progress. Start with some graph paper, or draw evenly spaced horizontal and vertical lines to make a grid. Next put a time line along the bottom — how many weeks or months (or even years) you're going to save for something. Then add some money levels along the left side, with the top level as your savings goal. If you have a computer handy, you can create the same type of savings graph using a spreadsheet program. Here's how Maida Money's savings graph looked when she wanted to save $100 for a new snowboard:

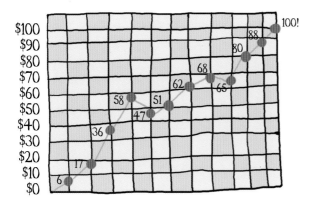

Each month Maida put a dot where the month and the amount of money she had saved crossed. Then she joined the dot with a line to the dot from the month before. See how the graph line sometimes goes down instead of up? Those were times when some unexpected expenses came up, so Maida spent some of her savings, which was okay because she knew she would make it up later.

CHART IT

Another even simpler way to keep track is to make a money thermometer, or bar chart.

Draw a long, thin rectangle. Next add some money levels along the side, with the top level as your savings goal, just like in the savings graph. Then as your dollars add up, fill in the thermometer with a red marker.

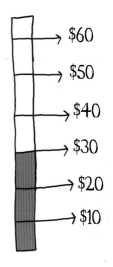

Put the funky in functional save-it jars

A quick and easy way to stash your cash and to keep track of what you're saving is to make a low-tech savings account, also known as ... a jar. If you're saving for something special, glue a picture of it on one side of the jar. Then, to keep track of how much you've saved, glue a money thermometer to the other side. Fill in the money thermometer with a marker to keep track of your savings as you add to the jar.

Bank on it

Once you've got a little stash together, it's a great idea to open a bank account. It'll help you save by keeping your money out of sight, and — get this! — the bank will actually pay you to keep your money there.

Getting your own account

Opening a bank account is a worry-free way of keeping your money safe. When you open a bank account, it's in your name. The bank has its own lingo, so here are a few terms you should know.

Balance: the amount of money in your bank account

Deposit: the amount of money you put into your account at any one time

Withdrawal: the amount of money you take out of your account at any one time

Transaction: any deposit or withdrawal of money from your account, including the use of checks and bank cards

Just like looking for a great bargain at the mall, you should shop around for the best bank deal before you open an account. Check out regular banks as well as credit unions and community banks. Most banks have helpful Web sites that can give you the scoop, but you can also drop in and ask for a personal tour. (You might even get to see the giant safe!) Here are some questions to ask the people at the bank before you open an account:

✱ *Do you have a special account for young people?*

✱ *Does an adult have to co-sign to open an account? Will that adult have access to the money in my account?*

✱ *What interest rate do you offer?* Depending on the type of account you have, the interest rate might range between 1 to 4%. (See page 40 for why higher is better.)

✱ *How much money do I have to deposit to open an account?*

✱ *Are there any fees charged for having an account?* Shop around for a free account.

✱ *Are there any penalties or charges for making small deposits?* There shouldn't be!

✱ *Will I get a bank card to use at the bank machine? Is there a fee if I use it at another bank's machine? How much?*

✱ *Will I be able to look at my account online? Are there any fees for this?*

✱ *Will I get checks with my account?* A check is a written order to your bank to give money to someone. So if you write your mom a check for $15 and she cashes it, the bank will pay her $15 from your account. If you do get a checking account, ask your folks or someone from the bank to show you how to fill out a check properly.

✱ *How many free transactions can I make every month? How much do you charge for each transaction after the free ones?*

✱ *Are there any fees for closing my account?* Find out if you have to pay to take out all your money or move it to another bank. Not every bank will charge you.

What's so INTEREST-ing about banking?

The best part about socking your savings away at the bank is that they actually pay you to keep it there. (The bank is borrowing your cash, and then they invest it, along with the money that everyone else deposits, to make more money.) The money the bank pays you is called interest. Your account will have an interest rate, or a percentage of interest, that will be paid to your account every year that you have money in it. The bank will divide the interest by twelve months and pay you $1/12$ a month. And even though the interest rate might seem low — around 4% — it can really add up! Here's how it works:

Say you put $100 in a bank account with a 4% interest rate. Just multiply $100 by 4% and you'll figure out that at the end of the first year, you'll get $4 interest just for keeping your money in there. That's four bucks for doing nothing! Can't beat that! Now you have $104.

But here's what's really interesting about interest: The $100 you put in to start, plus any other money you deposit, is called the principal. Once you start getting interest, you'll earn interest on that interest. Banks call this compound interest — you can just call it a good deal. Confused? Don't be! Check it out:

Now that you have $104, the next year you'll get interest on the original $100 and interest on the $4 interest you earned last year. So you'll have $104 x 4% = $4.16 interest + $104 = $108.16. The year after that, you'll get interest on $108.16, which is $4.32, and that adds up to $112.48. So in 3 years, you'll have made $12.48 without having had to lift a finger. Cha-ching!

The rule of 72

Don't worry, this isn't some weird list of 72 rules you have to follow! The rule of 72 is a cool way to figure out how long it will take for your bank balance to double. All you have to do is divide the number 72 by your account's interest rate, and what you get is how many years it will take to double your money. To figure out how long it will take for your original $100 to become $200 at a 4% interest rate:

$$72 \div 4 = 18 \text{ YEARS}$$

This may seem like a long time, but if you keep adding to your savings account, in eighteen years, you'll have double whatever you put in. This just goes to show how important it is to start saving as soon and as often as you can — and to shop around for a good interest rate before you open your account. Because remember, your money will double and you won't have to do a thing!

And if you save up a sweet little stash o' cash, think about putting it into a term deposit or buying a savings bond. You do have to have a minimum amount of money to do this, and your money is locked in for a certain amount of time (so you can't get at it), but you will get a higher rate of interest as a payoff. Check with your local bank for the scoop.

Picture frame wall safe

Create a secret stash for your cash that looks like just another pretty picture. Only you will know that your moolah is tucked in behind safe and sound!

- an 18 cm x 23 cm x 5 cm (7 in. x 9 in. x 2 in.) wood or cardboard cigar box (from a craft-supply or cigar store)
- a piece of Velcro 2.5 cm (1 in.) wide
- a 23 cm x 28 cm (9 in. x 11 in.) unfinished wood picture frame with glass, with a 13 cm x 17 cm (5 in. x 7 in.) center opening
- a picture for the frame
- 3M Command Picture Hanging Strips
- a glue gun and glue sticks
- newspaper, masking tape, craft paint, a small paintbrush
- a ruler, a pencil, a utility or craft knife, scissors

1 On one short end of the cigar box, measure and mark 7 cm (2½ in.) from each short edge. Then measure and mark 2 cm (¾ in.) from each long edge. Using a ruler, connect these marks to draw a rectangle.

2 Using the utility knife, carefully cut out the rectangle from step 1 to make a slot. Ask an adult to stand by to help you, and make sure you keep your fingers out of the way of the knife blade.

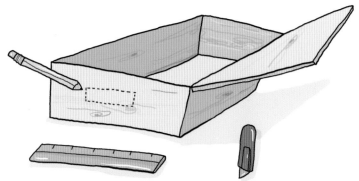

3 Separate the two sides of the Velcro. Cut one side in half and set the pieces aside.

4 Measure and mark the center point on the long edge of the mouth of the box. Glue one of the short pieces of Velcro to the side of the box at this point. Glue the long piece of Velcro to the inside lid of the box so that it wraps around the edge of the lid and sticks to the shorter piece on the side of the box.

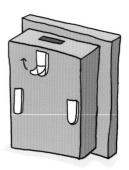

5 Remove the back of the picture frame, put your picture in, and replace the back of the frame. Apply a generous amount of glue to the cigar box lid. Center and stick the picture frame to the lid, with the top of the picture and the slot you made in step 2 at the same end.

6 Cover your work surface with newspaper. Apply masking tape around the inside edge of the picture frame glass to keep from getting paint on the glass.

7 Paint the picture frame and the cigar box the same color. Let dry. Repeat.

8 Apply the hanging strips to the back of the box, and then ask an adult to help you hang your wall safe. Tuck your money into the top slot, and when you want to make a withdrawal, lift the Velcro tab to crack the safe!

SPEND IT

A girl and her money are soon parted ...

There's nothing quite like spending your very own cashola on some new stuff. You've gotta love that feeling when you're skipping out of a shop, snappy shopping bag in hand. But you know how we were talking earlier about buyer's remorse, that feeling you have after you've bought something that wasn't the deal you thought it was? Something that wasn't quite so spiffy once you got it home? Check out this section for some handy tips on how to be a smart and savvy shopper, how to hush that "buy it!" voice in your head, and how to not get duped by fancy commercials that promise a whole new you if you just buy that fab new hair gloss. You're the one in charge of your money, and you've got a lot of power in that little wallet of yours.

QUIZ: What's your spending style?

Take this quiz to find out how you are at spending your money — penny wise or pound foolish?

1. Your best pal loves to spend Saturdays cruising for new clothes, lunching, sipping lattes. All very fun, but she gets twice as much allowance as you do, and these Super Saturdays are kind of pricey for you. You:

a) Go along for the ride. What's life without the good times?

b) Say forget it and start shopping around for a new friend instead.

c) Brainstorm some other fun plans for the two of you, and turn the Saturday spree into a monthly treat.

2. Your fave star launched a sassy new perfume. You:

a) Crack open your piggy bank. It's big bucks, but the ads say the star wears it all the time.

b) Don't even think about it. Your regular soap smells nice enough and you're not spending any money that you don't absolutely have to.

c) Add it to your wish list. You'll save up for a little while, and if you still want it later on, you'll go for it.

3. You spotted a fantastic pair of jeans, but they cost twice as much as your usual brand. You:

a) Skip going out with your friends for a few weeks to pay for them. It's worth it to look so darn good!

b) Keep wearing the same old pair you've had for two years. So they're a little hole-y ...

c) Check out some other stores to see if you can find a similar pair for less money. They may not be quite as hot, but they'll be easier on your wallet.

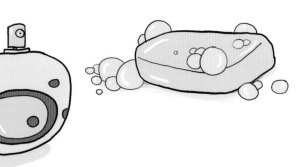

4. Your dream mp3 player is on sale for 20% off today only. You've been saving up for it, but you're only halfway there. You:

a) Buy it today through the store's payment plan. They don't charge too much interest.

b) Don't even consider it. You'll buy it when you have the money, sale or no sale.

c) Wrack your brain for a way to make it work. Maybe your parents would give you an advance on your future allowance? Hmm ...

5. You've had a rotten week at school (failed a test, urgh!), and to top it off, you had a fierce fight with your favorite sister. You:

a) Hop the bus to the mall. You need some retail therapy! There's nothing a new pair of shoes can't fix.

b) Retreat to your room to wallow in your misery. Why even try to make this nightmare of a week any better?

c) Rent a movie and splurge on a couple cupcakes. Then invite your sister to join you as an attempt to make peace.

ANSWERS

Mostly As: Sorry to tell you, but you're a silly spender. When you see something you want, you think it over for about, oh, two seconds, before you splurge. You're thinking only with your heart — and riding a one-way ticket to Brokeville.

Mostly Bs: You make Scrooge look like a spendthrift. It's great to be money wise, but don't forget to have some fun once in a while. Sometimes you gotta give a little to get a little.

Mostly Cs: Hey there, savvy spender! You're using your head and your heart. You're smart about what you buy, and you have a good time, too.

Think first, spend second

Being a money maven doesn't mean that you shouldn't spend your money — I mean, who doesn't love a little shopping now and then? — but there's a smart way to shop and a not-so-smart way to shop. You know that feeling you get when you've done something dumb? You know, like flunked a test 'cuz you didn't study, said something kinda mean to a friend, lost something important? Well, shopping smart means that you won't get home, open your shopping bags and get that icky feeling, that case of buyer's remorse.

The thing is, though, we're all programmed to crave instant gratification — getting what we want right when we want it. But that little voice in our heads telling us to go for it isn't always offering the best advice. So watch out for those impulse buys. If you feel the urge to splurge coming on, try this: Step out of the store, put a little distance between you and the gotta-have-it thing, and figure out 1) whether you really want it, 2) whether you really need it and 3) if it's really worth it. You'll be surprised at how many gotta-have-it things turn into what-was-I-thinking things! Before you surrender your cents, run through the smart-buy checklist.

Smart-Buy Checklist

❏ Is it a want or a need? New shoes because your old ones are worn out is a need; new shoes because they're the coolest thing is a want.

❏ If it's a want, can you afford it? Do you have the money right now? If you spend it on this, will you still be able buy other important things?

❏ Are you getting value for your money? Is it good quality? Does the price match what you're getting for it?

❏ Are you buying it for an emotional reason? Did you have a bad day, do you feel less trendy than your best friend or do you want to fit into a group? It's a tempting quick fix, but think twice. You'll probably find that buying something won't solve the problem.

❏ Have you thought of the extra costs, like sales tax, shipping and handling fees if you're ordering by mail, by phone or online? And what about extras like batteries and accessories, and even the bus fare to get to the store and back?

Pals or pressure?

Like they say, the best things in life — like good times with friends — are free. But it can be hard having less than other people (especially if they're your best pals). Having no money when everyone else seems to have lots can make you feel lousy. That's because of something called relative wealth, which is just a fancy way of saying "how much money one person has compared to someone else." No matter where you are in life, there will always be someone who has more than you and someone who has less. The best way to deal with that feeling is to try to be happy with what you have and not worry so much about everyone else.

If your best bud has money to burn and you're counting the coins you found under the sofa cushions, try to remember that it's way cooler to be able to tell a hilarious story than to sport the latest style. Or that you can have tons more fun laughing your butts off going through your closets making new outfits from your old faves than shopping your butts off and going broke at the mall.

Having a little less to work with is a chance to be creative. Be the one with fab but cheap ideas for doing fun stuff and you'll never feel left out. Invite a pile of pals over for a movie night instead of breaking the bank going out to the movies. (Another bonus? Scream as loud as you want when you're watching horror flicks!) Or skip the pricey trip to the ski hill and go for some old-fashioned tobogganing at the local hilly park — followed by hot cocoa at home, of course! Whether you're in the money or not, really great times can't be bought.

Shopping: The basics

At some point or another, though, we all need (yes, need) to do some shopping. There are lots of different types of stores, so here's the retail rundown.

✱ **Bricks-and-mortar stores:** This just means that it's a real store that you can go into because it's, you know, made of bricks and mortar. Make sure it's a shop you can trust. Has it been around for a while? Do you know other people who have shopped there and been happy with the customer service and what they bought? Do the salespeople make you feel welcome?

✱ **Online retailers:** There are tons of shopping Web sites, but it pays to be careful where you shop online. Make sure you get your parents' permission first. Then ask yourself the same questions you would for a bricks-and-mortar shop, and also: How do they accept payment? Is it secure? Will they give your information to anyone else? Will they let you return something? How long will it take to receive your purchase? If there are shipping and handling costs, how much do they add to the price of the item? Could you go to a real store and save these costs?

✱ **Second-hand shops:** Buying vintage (a fancy way of saying second-hand clothes) is a great way to get cool stuff without paying big-ticket prices. It also means you're less likely to end up in the same outfit as three other girls in your class. Even better, you're also helping out the environment by recycling something that's perfectly good instead of sending it to a landfill. But buyer beware. Give items a careful once-over before you buy. And if you're getting a crazy good deal, make sure you can get a guarantee so you don't get stuck with your purchase if you realize it's flawed or broken only after you get home.

51

✱ Dollar and discount stores: The prices are super cheap in these stores, but sometimes the products are super cheaply made, too. These stores are great for wrapping paper and cards, school and art supplies, and other bits and pieces, but make sure you take a really close look before you buy anything to make sure the quality is good enough for you. You know what they say: You get what you pay for. Plus, if the products are so cheap, do you think the workers who made them earned much money for their hard work?

Ticket to freedom

You know that little slip of paper that the cashier chucks into the bag when you buy something? That receipt is your ticket to freedom. Why? Because without it, you won't be able to return something you later decide you don't want or that doesn't quite fit. Put receipts in a safe place right away. Instead of leaving them in the bag and risking losing them, take them from the cashier and put them right into your wallet or purse. When you get home, keep them all in one place, like in an envelope pinned to your bulletin board or in your money journal.

But before you buy anything, make sure you know what the store's return policy is: Do you get a refund or store credit, or can you only make an exchange? What's the time limit on returns? If they don't accept returns, think long and hard about that purchase — go back to the smart-buy checklist on page 49. Is it really worth it?

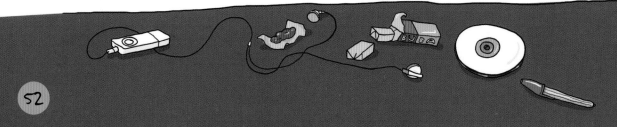

Deal or no deal?

Want to make sure you're getting a good deal for your money? Be a thrifty girl and be proud of it! Don't just buy something at the first place you see it. Do some comparative shopping research first to see what's out there. Look at flyers in the paper, check out online flyer sites with your parents, and ask people if they know the inside scoop. Be smarter than the stores think you are by knowing exactly what you're buying and how much it's really worth. Keep an eye out for sales and save big-ticket purchases for seasonal sale times like after holidays. And be a coupon clipper for toiletries and other things you have to buy anyway. (But don't be lured into buying something you don't need or really want

by the idea of saving a few dollars.) Make the grade and ask if there are student discounts. Lots of events, theaters and museums offer lower rates for students. (School can pay off in more ways than one!)

On the flip side, there are times when a bargain isn't really a bargain. When a store offers a sale or has stuff piled on a sale rack, they're not trying to do you a favor. What they're really doing is trying to get rid of stuff that didn't sell at full price. So ask yourself why it

didn't sell. Did they just order too many of something? Or did other people figure out that the product wasn't so great and either didn't go for it or returned it? In other words, is the quality questionable? When you do buy something on sale, try checking back at the store a week or two later. If the price is reduced even more, some stores will refund you the difference if it's within a couple of weeks of when you bought it. (Another good reason for saving those receipts!)

A Shopping Dilemma

Maida Money was looking through her T-shirt collection and realized that her favorite top was looking really tired — it (gasp!) even had a hole in the armpit — so she hit the shopping strip and here's what she found:

Store A: A super nice T-shirt by that hot new designer, good quality, excellent design, but a little pricey — forty bucks!

Store B: A nice quality T-shirt, locally made, 100% cotton — one for $25, or three for the price of two. So three T-shirts for $50 ($16.67 each).

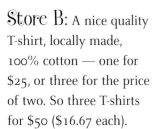

Store C: A real steal! Five T-shirts for $25, but you have to buy five at a time. Not such great quality, but they look good and Maida could have a whole new T-shirt wardrobe.

What's a girl to do? Maida has $25 to spend, so Store A's fab $40 designer T is out. Anyway, she's not into paying for the designer's name, and she knows that's really why it's so expensive. The deal at Store C seems amazing, but if the T-shirts fall apart in a few washes, it won't be much of a deal after all. And Maida's gotta wonder if there's any other reason why they're so cheap — were the workers at the factory where they were made treated fairly and paid enough? So that leaves Store B. She likes the Ts there and knows they'll hold up to a hundred washes, but should she go for the three-for-the-price-of-two deal? Is it really a deal when she needs only one T, not three? Eureka! Maida calls Penny Pincher to see if she wants in on the deal, and she does — they'll make great birthday presents for her twin sisters! So, Maida buys one T-shirt and Penny buys the other two — Maida gets a good deal, and Penny gets two really nice Ts for $33 and some change. That's two T-rific bargains in one!

Workers' rights or wronged workers?

When you're shopping, there's more to think about than what you want and whether you can afford it. You've probably noticed that you can get some of the same stuff for more or less money. For example, an umbrella at a department store might cost $30, and a similar umbrella might cost only $3 at a discount shop. There could be a difference in the quality of the materials used to make the umbrella, but sometimes other reasons are behind big price differences. Sadly, there are workers all over the world who are treated unfairly so that products can be made and sold very cheaply. Some workers have no health care, work very long hours in unsafe conditions and don't get paid for working overtime. Some of those workers are kids just like you, and some don't get paid at all — worse, they don't have a chance to go to school, either. The most frustrating part is that large companies and corporations often make gobs of money by treating their workers so badly.

So, what can you do about it? Think about what you're buying and where it came from. Do some research about the stores and brands you like and make sure they're treating their workers well. And if they're not, instead of giving them your cash, write or call them with your two cents' worth!

Don't be wooed

Girls your age spend lots and lots of money every year. Big companies have figured this out, and they do everything they can to take advantage of it — and you! They find out what you like and then create advertising to target you — yes, you! — so don't be a sitting duck.

Just knowing that you're being targeted should make you think twice about what ads are really telling you. Take a sec and think about that new soft drink commercial, for example. What kind of music did they use? Does it make the product sound really cool? What are the actors or characters doing, wearing and saying? Do they seem happy? Does what's

going on have anything to do with what the product really is about? And what about the celebrities you see doing ads — do they really love the product, or are they just getting a ton of cash to promote it? Also watch out for ads that show a lot of other stuff you have to buy separately from the product. What do you really get for

your money versus what they are showing you in the ad or on the package? If there's fine print, read it!

It costs a lot of money to make ads, commercials and fancy packaging. Do you know who's actually paying for it? When you buy one of those products, you are! Sometimes the price of an item is based more on how much the advertising costs than on how much it cost to make the item.

When you're in a store, think about what the store is doing to make you want to buy. Decorating with celebrity posters? Playing cool music? Making sure you have to walk all the way through the store, past all those displays of really cool and very tempting stuff, when you're just trying to get to the exit?

Sneaky Petes

Think you're a good ad spotter? Advertising isn't always in your face. Advertisers have figured out that they can get to you subconsciously by advertising in sneaky places. Keep your eyes open for these covert spots:

✽ ads in video games, like the name of a company on a flag in the background of a race track

✽ ads on clothes, like a company's name as part of the funky design on a hoodie or on the butt of your jeans

✽ names of buildings, like a sports stadium named after a soft drink or an insurance company

✽ product placements in movies and TV shows, like a brand of cereal on the counter in the movie-set kitchen or a scene shot at a particular coffee chain

✽ ads on other products, like an upcoming movie advertised on a soft drink cup or popcorn bag at the movie theatre

It's tough to get away from advertising. So be smart about the messages you read — be a consumer who thinks for herself.

Budgeting: Not so bad!

True, budgeting could easily be a drag — who wants to count every penny and keep track of every stick of gum you buy? But a budget is really just a map of where your money is coming from — your income (yep, you've got income, just like your parents do) — and where it's going to — your expenses. And it can be quite enlightening when you get a bird's-eye view of your money sitch. Maybe you'll discover why you ran out of allowance last week or why you never seem to have any money for special treats. Budgeting means that you control your money, instead of your money controlling you.

First, figure out your income. You might not be earning a salary working 9 to 5, but do you get an allowance, do some babysitting or lawn mowing or get some money for a special occasion? Keep your eye on this money (remember Keeping Track on page 24 and Track Your Loot on page 36?) and you'll know what your income is.

Next, figure out your expenses. There are two types of expenses: fixed and variable. Fixed expenses are things you probably can't avoid and that come up regularly, like paying bus fare. Variable expenses are things you won't always know the cost of in advance or stuff that doesn't happen regularly, like buying a lunchtime treat or birthday gift.

Here's an example of what your budget could look like:

INCOME	$	EXPENSES	$
Allowance		Bus fare	
Babysitting		Lunch on Fridays	
Birthday gifts		Savings	
Money my brother owes me		Going out with friends	
		Clothing	
		Toiletries	
		School supplies	
		Cell phone	
		Magazines and books	
		Music	
		Money I owe Dad	
		Charitable donation	
TOTAL INCOME		TOTAL EXPENSES	

The trick to keeping your budget under control? If your income is the same or more than your expenses, congrats, you've made sense of your cents! But if your expenses are more than your income, you're headed for trouble. Time to trim those expenses — would it really kill you to bring a sandwich from home and skip buying lunch on Fridays?

Keep a money journal

The best way to keep track of your income and expenses is to get in the habit of keeping a money journal. You can jot down things as they happen or you can keep receipts and update it every week — whatever works for you. Be sure to date all of your entries and write down where and why you spent your money.

Why bother? Well, after a while you might start to see patterns, like maybe how you spend more on days when you're feeling blue. Are the things you bought on those days things you would have bought if you were in a better mood? You might notice that you spend way more money in one area — on your fab style, say — and less in another area — hanging out with your fab friends. Or you might notice that buying lunch at school a couple times a week seems like nothing at the time, but by month's end, you've spent $35! That's enough for that wicked new computer game you've been dying for. Ouch!

The deal with debt

Debt (money you owe someone else) is the same no matter whom you owe it to, right? Actually, there's good debt and bad debt. Bad debt is when you borrow money to buy something that won't go up in value, like new shoes.

You know how the bank pays you interest when you have money in a savings account? The same deal applies to you when you borrow money from the bank — only this time you're the one paying them the interest.

Using a credit card is one way of borrowing money. But credit cards charge you a lot more interest than a bank will ever pay you. When you use a credit card, you have the option to pay for what you bought at the end of the month, interest free. And if you always pay your balance in full and on time at the month's end, a credit card can be very useful — for buying things online, for example. But when you carry a balance (don't pay your credit card bill in full), the credit card company charges you interest on that balance for each day it isn't paid. Some credit cards charge as much as 28% annual interest! So if you charge your $54.00 shoes to a 28% interest credit card, the shoes will have cost you $69.12 a year later. Not such a great bargain in the end, especially if they're all worn out already!

Another way of borrowing money is through store credit. Some stores offer payment plans so that you can buy something and pay for it in installments (a set amount that you pay at regular times). But just like credit cards, they charge you interest — and usually at a very high rate. And some stores won't allow you to pay more than the set installment amount. So even if you get the money to pay for your purchase in full, they won't let you because then you would be paying them less money in interest. The only one that wins with store credit is the store, so it's much better to save up the money to pay for something in cash.

Good debt is when you borrow money to pay for something that will go up in value. Borrowing money to pay for your education is always a good idea — you'll get brighter and so will your future. Look into special student loans offered by some banks and through government programs. They usually have low interest rates and easy repayment plans. (And don't forget to check into bursaries, prizes and scholarships that award money to deserving students.) You'll make enough money from that education to help you pay back the money you borrowed to get it — and much more! Further down the road, borrowing money to buy a house or a condo will definitely make your home life sweet. While you're paying the house loan (called a mortgage) back, you'll have a roof over your head. And if all goes well, by the time you pay it all back, the house will be worth much more than what you paid for it.

So before you dive into the debt pool or get lured by a credit card company's slick ads or a store's payment plan, think about whether the debt will be good or bad. Remember, if a deal sounds too good to be true, it usually is.

Spending: How not to!

A big part of smart spending is deciding when not to spend. Before you buy anything, think about the opportunity costs (O.C.). An O.C. is what you give up because you choose to do or buy something else. Say you want to get a season's pass to Rollercoaster World. But if you do, you won't be able to get the newest model of that gaming system you want so much — the O.C. of a summer full of loop-de-loops is not getting the new gaming system.

You'll probably find that your first impulse is to just buy something you want — that's what our society teaches us — but there are alternatives to spending money. Here are some great ways to be a smart saver:

✽ Have a clothes, book or CD swap. It feels like getting new stuff, but it won't cost a penny. Get a bunch of your gal pals together and make it a party. (Donate leftover items to charity shops and share the wealth!)

✽ Cook or bake stuff instead of buying it. What could be sweeter than spending your time instead of your money?

✽ Go to the library instead of the bookstore. You can even order books you want through the librarian or on the library's Web site, and you'll get a call when the books arrive at your local branch.

✽ Make gifts. You'll be surprised at how many simple but gorgeous things you can make yourself. Look online and in mags and books for creative ideas and then make them at a fraction of the cost.

✽ Give your time. Make a coupon or a whole book of coupons as a gift for someone. Betcha your parents would love a coupon promising to bathe the dog every weekend for a month, clean out the garage or do some weeding!

63

Stash-it shopping bag

Strut your stuff in style! Skip those bad-for-the-Earth plastic shopping bags and make this super durable, super stashable ripstop fabric bag.

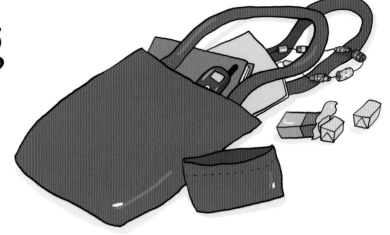

STUFF YOU NEED

- 1 m (1 yd.) lightweight ripstop fabric
- 1 m (1 yd.) of 2.5 cm (1 in.) wide grosgrain ribbon or strapping
- a sewing needle or a sewing machine
- thread to match the fabric
- a tape measure, a pencil, scissors, pins

1 Measure, mark and cut a 35 cm x 80 cm (14 in. x 32 in.) piece of ripstop fabric.

2 Fold the fabric in half lengthwise. Pin and then sew a 1 cm (1/2 in.) seam along the two longer edges, leaving the short edge open for the top. Remove the pins.

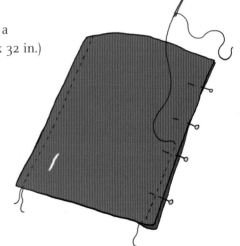

3 Turn the bag right side out. Fold the open edges toward the inside of the bag 2.5 cm (1 in.) twice, pinning as you go. Sew a 1 cm ($^1/_2$ in.) hem around the opening, removing the pins as you go.

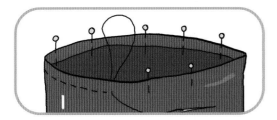

4 For the handles, measure, mark and cut two 60 cm (24 in.) pieces of ribbon.

5 On one side of the bag, pin the ends of one strap to the inside top edge, 2.5 cm (1 in.) below the opening and 10 cm (4 in.) from each edge. Sew the handle securely in place by making a box as shown. Remove the pins.

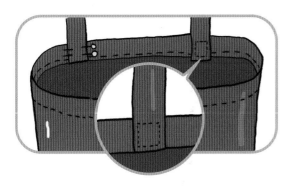

6 Repeat step 5 to sew the second handle to the other side of the bag.

7 To make the carrying case, measure, mark and cut a 15 cm x 25 cm (6 in. x 10 in.) piece of ripstop fabric.

8 Fold the fabric in half widthwise. Pin and then sew a 1 cm ($^1/_2$ in.) seam along one short edge and the longer open edge.

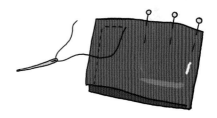

9 Turn the case right side out. Fold the open edges toward the inside of the case 1 cm ($^1/_2$ in.) twice, pinning as you go. Sew a 0.5 cm ($^1/_4$ in.) hem around the opening. Remove the pins. Now fold up your bag, tuck it in the case and stash it somewhere handy for when you need it!

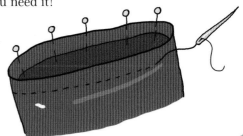

SHARE IT

Share and share alike

Money, money, money. Now that you know all about making it, saving it and spending it, there's another great way to make your money matter — sharing it! Giving money to a good cause is one of the best investments you'll make because your return will be in the good feelings you have about yourself, and we all know you can't put a price on that. Sure, you're just one girl with a limited amount of cash ... what difference can you make? Lots, actually. Even the smallest money donation will make a difference to your favorite charity or nonprofit. But if money's too tight to mention, fundraising and volunteering are great ways to give back to the community, too. Wanna make this world a better place? This section has lots of tips for making your mark.

QUIZ: How much do you care to share?

Just how generous you are with your time and money? Take this quick quiz to find out!

1. At school, every class is asked to think of ways to raise some funds to help your sister school buy new textbooks. You put up your hand and:

a) Actually, you don't put up your hand. Of course you care, but right now you've got your own money worries.

b) Suggest collection jars for the caf, library and main office. For sure people will dig deep into their pockets!

c) Suggest that your school hold a Fun Fair, and volunteer for the dunking booth. Why not do some good and have fun at the same time?

2. There's a new donation box by the cash at your favorite juice bar. You:

a) Notice it but are too busy making sure they gave you the correct change to ask what it's all about.

b) Are happy to see that someone else cares about the things you do. You buy a small juice instead of the medium and put the extra money in the box.

c) Are happy to see that someone else cares about the things you do. You make a note of the charity's name to find out if they need local volunteers.

3. You and your friends are asked to take part in a fundraiser to help find the cure for a serious childhood illness. You:

a) Wish you could, but you're working that day.

b) Are happy to give some of your babysitting money to the cause.

c) Get to work making your famous When-life-gives-you-lemons lemonade to sell at the event.

4. Your best bud is in a bowl-a-thon to raise money for an organization that builds homes for people who can't afford to buy a house. You:

a) Go down to the bowling alley to cheer her on.

b) Sponsor her and go down to the bowling alley to cheer for her.

c) Join her team and start looking for your own sponsors.

5. Your b-day is coming up, and your parents are throwing you a huge bash. On the invites you:

a) Write about how sooo very excited you are for the party.

b) Include the Web site address of your favorite charity and ask people to make donations in your name instead of buying you a gift.

c) Organize a food drive by asking people to bring canned and dry goods for the food bank instead of buying you a gift.

ANSWERS

Mostly As: You work hard for your money, but maybe it's time to think about sharing some of it.

Mostly Bs: You're putting your money where your mouth (and heart) is.

Mostly Cs: If time = money, you're the female Bill Gates!

Giving: It's not just for the holidays

Helping those in need is always in style. Just look at all those celebs who turn up at fundraising events and hand over one of those gigantic (and kinda silly-looking) checks. Of course, as much as you give or do, you probably won't get the same kind of attention. But you know what? It doesn't take paparazzi and roaring crowds to feel like you've done a good thing.

Ever offered your seat to an older person on the bus? Or held the door open for someone struggling with an armload of groceries? Those little acts of kindness feel pretty darn good to the person you've helped and to you, too. The same thing is true about giving even a little of your money and time. What might seem like a small thing to you can mean something much bigger to someone who needs a little help.

If you think about it, making a donation is money and time well spent. Here's why: Say you decide to give $10 to the local animal shelter. Your contribution might go toward buying food for the animals. You know that you're helping keep the animals comfortable and well fed — already that's a lotta bang for your buck. And when you give your money, the shelter can spend some of the money that was going toward buying food on something else that helps them take care of the animals, like repairs to their walking yard. When a donation leaves your pocket, it takes on a life of its own! Same thing with the time you give — a little goes a much longer way than you might realize. If you volunteer as a dog walker for the shelter, not only are you bringing some happiness to a pup's day, but that's one less thing the shelter has to pay someone to do. Like with cash donations, that means they'll have more money to put toward the other things the animals need.

Mission possible

Think there's not much that one girl can do to change the world? Think again.

Way back in 2001, when Hannah Taylor was in first grade in Winnipeg, Manitoba, she decided she had to turn the worry and sadness she felt when she saw homeless people into something positive. Her class had an art and bake sale, and from that, they donated hundreds of cans of coffee, warm clothes and blankets to the local homeless shelter. A great first effort, but Hannah wanted to do more. She painted 300 empty baby food jars with ladybugs (her fave creature and a symbol of good luck) and asked local businesses to put them out to collect people's spare change. This was the beginning of the Ladybug Foundation, an organization that raises both money and awareness, and now has support from all across Canada. So far $1 million has been raised for shelters and food banks, and she's not stopping there! (You can find out just how well she's doing by visiting www.ladybugfoundation.ca.) Talk about making (spare) change happen!

Hannah figured out that a small start has the potential to grow, grow, grow. What begins as a one-time fundraising event can become a yearly event or even a monthly one. If you're passionate about it, your own project can expand to include your family, friends, school, community, city ... and, who knows, someday maybe even the world!

Choosing your charity

Giving your money and time is good, but giving wisely is even better. The first step to becoming a wise-gal giver is figuring out what cause you want to help.

First, think about what you'd like to change about this crazy world. If nothing jumps to mind right away, you can get more informed by following the news in the paper or online, on TV or on the radio. Talk to your friends and family about their fave causes. What about checking out groups at school that are organized around a special cause, like the environment or homelessness?

Next, make a list of your concerns. You can include things that affect you directly, like the lack of trees in your downtown, and big issues that seem a bit farther away, like world hunger. Be warned: You might find yourself with a pretty long list. Don't get freaked out — the list is just to help you decide what concerns you the most. It might be an easy decision or it might take you some time to decide. The important thing to remember is that you'll be most helpful if you focus on only one or two causes. If everyone did this, eventually our world would be the place we want it to be!

Now that you've chosen your cause, you've gotta do your research to find the right charity (an organization set up to help those in need or support a particular issue or belief). The goal of the charity can be to raise money, raise awareness, provide help or any combination of those three things. Charities run mainly on volunteer help, and any money they make goes into running the charity and to the cause that it's helping. Here are some things to find out about an organization from its Web site and brochures or by writing or calling them. (No need to feel shy — it's your money and time, so it's your right!)

✴ What exactly do they do to help the cause? You want to be sure that your beliefs are the same as the charity's and that you agree with the way they work.

✴ How much of the money donated goes to the cause you're supporting? Some of the money might need to go to the costs of running the organization, but if a charity is worthy of your support, 60% or more of donations should go directly to the work that it does.

✴ If you're planning to donate your time, find out what the organization needs in the way of volunteers. Do they need only people with special training? Is there an age requirement? Do the hours that they would need you for fit in with your schedule? Is the organization close to home?

Also check out Web sites that list registered charities (ones that are recognized by the government). But to be on the safe side, if you or your folks have never heard of a particular charity, it's wise not to give money until you know for sure it's legit. This might sound harsh, but there are some people who will try to take advantage of generosity.

Putting your money where your heart is

Being the cents-ible girl that you are, it can be pretty easy to make giving a part of your money plan. Remember that 10% solution from page 32? Think about using some of the money you've put aside for your fave charity either by donating every month or even by saving up for a once-a-year donation. Or if you're a girl entrepreneur, why not make it your business to donate a percentage of the money you make to a cause? (Be sure to include this info in your ads — you might even find yourself with more customers as a result. Talk about a win-win situation!) Being money smart is pretty powerful stuff, especially when it means you can help others as well as yourself.

Once you're sure the charity is on the up and up (and we just can't stress that enough), there are a few ways you can donate. If the organization has an office close by, you and your parents can drop off cash or a check. If you're mailing in your donation, write a check rather than sending cash through the mail. This way, if there's a problem with the donation, the bank can help you trace the check. Don't have your own checking account? Give your parents the money and ask them to write the check to the charity from their account. Some charities let you make donations right on their Web sites, either by debit card or credit card — just be sure to clear it with your folks first. If you don't have your own credit card or debit card, you can ask your parents to do it and give them the money.

There are no rules when it comes to how much you should give. The fact that you're giving at all makes you a hero. If you feel any pressure to donate more money or more often than you can, don't be afraid to say no. And if a charity sends you something in the mail that you didn't ask for, like postcards or a calendar, don't feel like you owe them a donation. Lots of good organizations are in need, but your guilt shouldn't get the better of you. Knowing your limit is also part of giving wisely. Really feeling the pressure? Call or e-mail the charity and ask them to take your name off their contact list.

No matter how you make your donation or how much you give, make sure you get a receipt. Remember to track it in your money journal, too (see page 60). And hey, why not use a colored pen and some stickers when you record it? This kind of entry deserves some special treatment!

Charity

The fun of fundraising

Looking for another way to make a difference? Get fundraising! There are loads of ways to collect money or contributions for the cause.

Why not take Penny Pinchers's lead and ask people to make a donation in your name instead of giving you birthday gifts? Or if your special day is around the holidays, ask people to bring cans for the food bank or an unwrapped toy for a toy drive to your party. Now these are gifts that keep on giving.

If you like your theme parties, you're just the girl to think up a way to make money that relates to the organization. For example, say you hear that the local food bank is running low on supplies, and they need some help. You then decide to spend a week selling tickets for a guess at the number of oaty bits in an unopened cereal box. People buy a guess for a dollar or a canned good. The person that has the closest guess wins a prize donated by a local store. (Need to break a tie? Give the prize to the person who contributed the most.)

Part of a club or have a bunch of like-minded pals? A group event really puts the fun in fundraising. You might be surprised by how much money you can raise by having a garage or bake sale, a car wash or a fashion show.

How about a garage sale/bake sale/car wash/fashion show? On second thought, maybe not. When you're planning a fundraiser it's best to follow the KISS rule — Keep It Simple, Silly!

Girls just wanna raise funds

Like any party or event, a fundraiser needs a good plan. Here's a checklist to help you get organized for the big day. (You might have other things to add, so think of this as a starting point!)

Fabulous Fundraiser Checklist

❏ Do you have permission? You need your folks', and you'll need to get it from the people in charge where the event is taking place. When you make your pitch, go with info about the organization you're helping; belief in a good cause is catchy.

❏ Do you have your team? Figure out what you need help with and give everyone a specific job — this is key.

❏ Have you set a date? Even car washing takes planning, so give yourself time to prepare well and to spread the word. If you can, make sure there aren't any other events that day: No one needs the competition.

❏ Are you ready? You've got the people power, but what else will you need? Plenty of small bills and coins to make change? Folding tables? If the event is going to be more than a couple hours, think about snacks for your team. Try to keep your costs low: It might be time to call in some favors.

❏ Are you excited?! Any event can be a lot of work, so the more you're looking forward to it, the easier it will be. Plus, your team might need a boost now and then, so be ready to help keep their energy up. Being positive will also keep you going with the flow.

A LITTLE HELP?

If you need prizes or supplies, try getting help from local businesses: Ask to speak to the owner or manager. Look snappy, have a happy, can-do attitude and be prepared to give them all the important deets: who you are, what the charity is, and what and when the event is. Have your list of what you need set for when they agree to help. Put some thought into how you can advertise their support, too: You can list their help on your posters and flyers, thank them in a speech at the event, or if they have flyers of their own, offer to hand them out at the event. MOST IMPORTANTLY, follow the safety tips on page 25 when you go out into the community.

The follow-up

Once your event is over and everything is cleaned up, it's time to give yourself and everyone involved a huge pat on the back. You've worked hard and made a difference. And not only have you raised some money for something you believe in, but you've got others thinking about it, too. If you were a superhero, your superpower would be generosity!

Now, about those fundraised funds ... Two heads are better than one, so make sure you get two people to count the cash your event brought in. This way you'll be doubly sure that you have the correct amount. If you can, take the money you raised directly to the organization. Or even better, mail them a check. This way, if there's any problem with the donation, there's a way to track it. For some bigger charities, you can make the donation through their Web site, but you'll need to use a credit card or debit card. However you make the donation, be sure to get a receipt for your records.

Spread the good feelings about what you've done by letting people know how much money was raised. Put up posters, make announcements at school and ask the charity to post it on their Web site. Pay a visit or send a thank-you letter to any businesses that helped you out. They'll see that they've contributed to something and will be more likely to do so again if you have another event. They might even bring their friends!

Taking action

What's that saying? Time is money? Nothing could be truer when it comes to helping a worthwhile cause. Take some action and volunteer your time. Once you've got your parents' permission, finding the right volunteer gig is sort of like finding the right job, so think about the questions on pages 14 and 16 before you begin your search.

You might be surprised at how many ways there are to donate your time and talent. You've heard of fashionistas? Well, here are just a few suggestions for finding your inner *actionista*.

TALENT...	VOLUNTEER GIG ...
academics	after-school tutoring
acting	reading during story time at the public library
caring for animals	dog walking at the local shelter
gardening	joining a group that looks after public gardens and spaces
knitting or crocheting	making hats and blankets for newborn babies at the local hospital
making jokes or doing magic	clowning around at a children's hospital
singing or playing an instrument	entertaining at a seniors' residence
playing sports	becoming a volunteer coach
public speaking	becoming a speaker on behalf of a charitable organization
sewing	mending clothes and blankets for people living in homeless shelters

Not only is giving your time good for others, it's good for you, too. It's a great way to meet people and to get some experience. Your volunteer time at the local hospital might help you decide that you're destined for a career in medicine, or tending public gardens might lead to a career in landscape design. And even in the shorter term, if you're looking for a paying after-school or weekend job, a potential boss will be very impressed by the caring and commitment you show with your weekly visits to the seniors' residence or animal shelter.

When-life-gives-you-lemons lemonade

*Just the thing to offer to people waiting for
their car to be washed or to sell at the Fun Fair.*

STUFF YOU NEED

- 4 to 6 lemons to make 250 mL (1 c.) of juice
- 250 mL (1 c.) sugar
- 1250 mL (5 c.) cold water
- wax paper
- a knife
- a cutting board
- a juicer, measuring cup
- a small saucepan
- a wooden spoon
- a plastic juice container

1 Cut the lemons in half. Squeeze 4 to 6 lemons over a measuring cup to make 250 mL (1 c.) of juice. Set aside.

2 Measure the sugar and only 250 mL (1 c.) of water into the saucepan. Heat the mixture, stirring it until the sugar dissolves. (It doesn't need to boil.)

3 Pour the juice and the sugar-water mixture into the juice container.

4 Add the rest of the water and stir well. Pop it in the fridge for about an hour, and you're ready to go.

Serves 6 to 8, depending on cup size.

ADDED BONUS:

What's a better seller than homemade lemonade? Nothing, except maybe PINK homemade lemonade. Just follow the recipe for When-life-gives-you-lemons lemonade, but use 250 mL (1 c.) sweetened cranberry juice and 1 L (4 c.) water. For step 3, add the cranberry juice to the lemon juice and sugar-water mixture in the juice container.